Building A
New Land

African Americans in

Colonial America

James Haskins *and*
Kathleen Benson

illustrated by
James Ransome

HarperCollinsPublishers

 Amistad

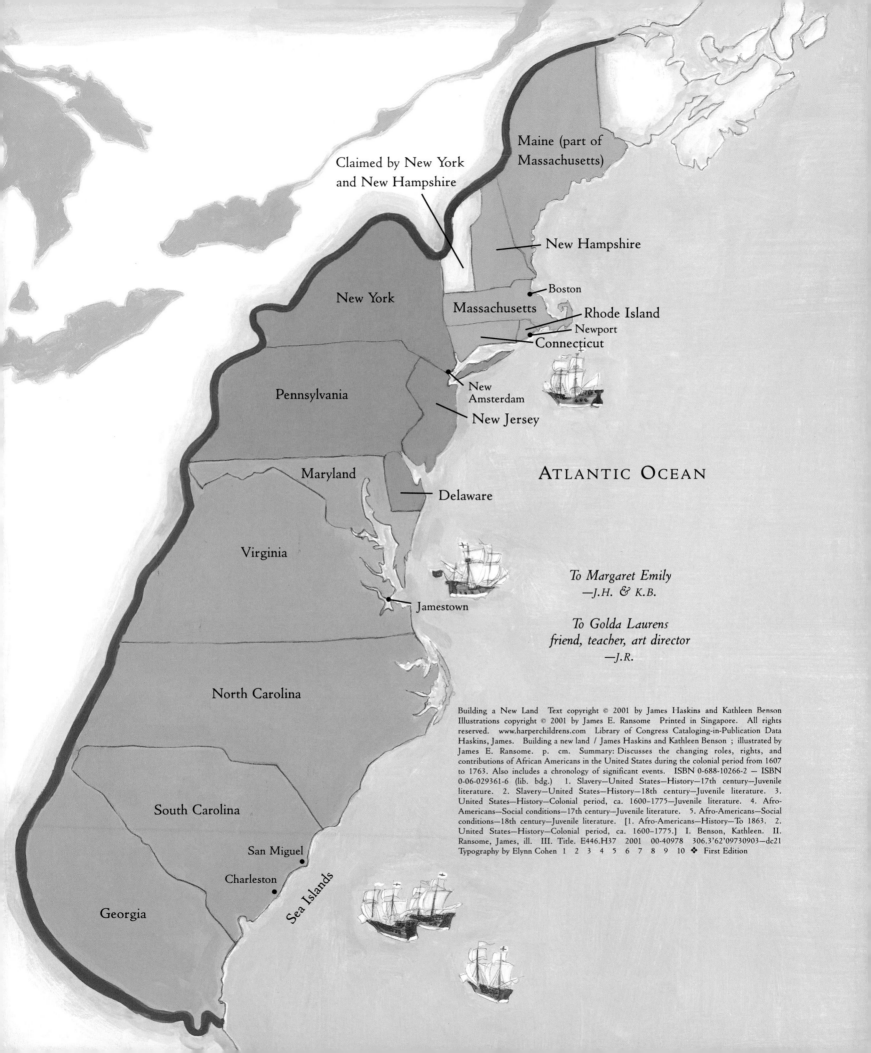

Maine (part of
Massachusetts)

Claimed by New York
and New Hampshire

New Hampshire

Boston

New York

Massachusetts

Rhode Island

Newport

Connecticut

Pennsylvania

New
Amsterdam

New Jersey

Maryland

Delaware

ATLANTIC OCEAN

Virginia

To Margaret Emily
—J.H. & K.B.

Jamestown

To Golda Laurens
friend, teacher, art director
—J.R.

North Carolina

South Carolina

Building a New Land   Text copyright © 2001 by James Haskins and Kathleen Benson
Illustrations copyright © 2001 by James E. Ransome   Printed in Singapore. All rights
reserved. www.harperchildrens.com Library of Congress Cataloging-in-Publication Data
Haskins, James.   Building a new land / James Haskins and Kathleen Benson ; illustrated by
James E. Ransome. p. cm. Summary: Discusses the changing roles, rights, and
contributions of African Americans in the United States during the colonial period from 1607
to 1763. Also includes a chronology of significant events.   ISBN 0-688-10266-2 — ISBN
0-06-029361-6 (lib. bdg.) 1. Slavery—United States—History—17th century—Juvenile
literature. 2. Slavery—United States—History—18th century—Juvenile literature. 3.
United States—History—Colonial period, ca. 1600–1775—Juvenile literature. 4. Afro-
Americans—Social conditions—17th century—Juvenile literature. 5. Afro-Americans—Social
conditions—18th century—Juvenile literature. [1. Afro-Americans—History—To 1863. 2.
United States—History—Colonial period, ca. 1600–1775.] I. Benson, Kathleen. II.
Ransome, James, ill. III. Title. E446.H37 2001 00-40978 306.3'62'09730903—dc21
Typography by Elynn Cohen 1 2 3 4 5 6 7 8 9 10 ❖ First Edition

San Miguel

Charleston

Sea Islands

Georgia

Contents

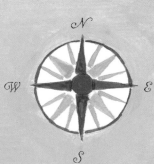

EUROPE

AFRICA

Before the *Mayflower*

African slaves were the largest single group of non-English-speaking people to enter the North American colonies before the Revolutionary War. The proportion of blacks to whites has never again been as high as it was during the eighteenth century. These blacks were pioneers: Whether free, servant, or slave, they were instrumental in building America.

Blacks accompanied the first Spanish, Portuguese, and French explorers. In 1492, a black Spaniard named Pedro Alonzo Niño was the navigator on the *Santa Maria*, one of Christopher Columbus's ships. Another black Spaniard, Diego Mendez, was a crew member on Columbus's 1502 voyage; and thirty African seamen sailed with Vasco Núñez de Balboa when he discovered the Pacific Ocean.

African slavery in the New World did not become established until after settlers from Spain, Portugal, France, and the Netherlands found that the Indians of the Caribbean islands and South America were ill-suited to slavery. Christopher Columbus tried to use Indian slaves to mine for gold, but they revolted. Realizing that there was not much gold to be found, Columbus started an Indian slave trade in hopes of making big profits. But hundreds of the slaves who were sent to Spain died during the voyage. They also died in huge numbers from diseases they contracted in Europe.

In 1517, the Spanish missionary and historian Bishop Bartolomé de Las Casas petitioned the Spanish crown to allow each Spanish settler in the Americas to import twelve enslaved Africans. Spain assented, and the Atlantic slave trade began.

The first African slaves to settle permanently in North America were those of Lucas Vásquez de Ayllón, who established a settlement called San Miguel at the site of present-day Georgetown, South Carolina, in 1526. Within a year, more than half the Spaniards died, and the Africans set fire to the settlement, escaped, and went to live with the Seminole Indians.

Slavery in English-speaking North America dates from 1619, when twenty Africans—including three women—arrived at Jamestown, Virginia, on a Dutch ship. They were put to work alongside English and Irish servants and Indian slaves. The law didn't define exactly what being a slave meant, and the Africans were regarded and treated like the European indentured servants with whom they lived and worked. The lines between free and slave—and between black, white, and Indian—had not yet been clearly drawn.

All of this activity occurred *before* 1620, when the *Mayflower* dropped anchor at Plymouth Rock in present-day Massachusetts.

Atlantic Creoles

In the early colonial years, people's roles in the new society were determined by whether or not they were Christians, rather than by their race. The first blacks to arrive in North America were variously navigators, laborers, freemen, indentured servants—and slaves. Some whites were free; others were indentured servants. Some Native Americans were enslaved, while others were not.

The term *Atlantic Creoles* has been used to describe the Africans of this period. An Atlantic Creole might have had African and European parents or might have been a full-blooded African, well-versed in his own traditions, who had experience with European languages, commerce, and culture.

Many Atlantic Creoles came from the west coast of Africa. European slave traders sometimes took African women as their mistresses. Many of their children used their knowledge of diverse languages and cultures to advantage, becoming skilled traders and acting as negotiators. The disadvantage of this mixed heritage was that they were not entirely trusted by either the Europeans or the Africans. Regarded as proud and haughty, many took advantage of the first opportunity to leave Africa, and over time they found their way to islands off the African coast, to the capitals of Europe, and eventually to the New World. Atlantic Creoles may have constituted the majority of the first twenty

blacks sold to the Jamestown settlers in 1619.

Many Atlantic Creoles who arrived in the North American colonies in the early years secured their freedom by escaping or by buying themselves out of slavery. They had opportunities to own land and could go to court if they felt their rights had been violated. But over the years, as the colonists discovered plantation agriculture and the demand for labor grew, slave traders began to import non-Creole Africans. Slavery and servitude became more closely identified with race, and the legal system began to preserve the rights of whites and to deprive blacks of theirs.

"Antonio, a Negro"

The story of Anthony Johnson illustrates the change over time in the position of most colonial blacks. His existence is first recorded in 1621, when a slave known as "Antonio, a Negro" was sold to the English at Jamestown. It is likely that he was familiar with European languages, Christianity, and other aspects of European culture.

He went to work on a plantation owned by a family named Bennett and was one of the few people who survived a 1622 Indian raid that nearly destroyed the Jamestown colony. Antonio was commended by the Bennetts for his "hard labor and known service." He was also given permission to marry a fellow slave named Mary and to baptize his children.

Eventually, Antonio won his freedom and took the name Anthony Johnson. When the Bennetts moved across the Chesapeake Bay to the eastern shore of Virginia, the Johnson family followed. There, the Johnsons established their own farm, where they grew tobacco and corn. In 1651, the Colony of Virginia granted Johnson two hundred fifty acres of land in return for his sponsorship of servants entering the colony. When his farm burned in 1653, Johnson got his taxes reduced so that he could rebuild his farm.

Like other planters in the Chesapeake region of Virginia, Anthony Johnson needed slaves to work his farm. In 1654, John Casar, one of Johnson's black

slaves, claimed his freedom and sought refuge with two neighboring white planters. Johnson went to court to get Casar back. The legal proceedings took a year, but eventually Johnson won Casar's return.

In 1665, in search of richer land, Anthony and Mary Johnson moved to Somerset County, Maryland, where they established a three-hundred-acre farm called Tonies Vineyard. Johnson deeded fifty of his Virginia acres to his son Richard. He paid for his move by selling his other two hundred acres on credit to two white planters, who promised to pay him in tobacco. Two years later, according to the agreement of sale, planter Edmund Scarburgh delivered 1,344 pounds of tobacco to the Somerset County sheriff as payment for Johnson's land.

But by this time, the attitude of white Virginia colonists toward the blacks in their midst had changed. The legal rights that free black men like Anthony Johnson had once enjoyed were slowly and steadily being taken away, and many whites seized the opportunity to take advantage of them.

Edmund Scarburgh saw a chance to keep his tobacco crop. He forged a letter in which Johnson promised to repay money to Scarburgh—a sum that matched the value of the tobacco Scarburgh had delivered. Authorities ignored the fact that Anthony Johnson could neither read nor write and decided in Scarburgh's favor. Johnson seems to have made no effort to challenge the court decision, and Scarburgh got his tobacco back.

After Johnson's death in 1670, an all-white jury ruled that his original land in Virginia could be seized by the colony "because he was a Negroe and by consequence an alien." The two hundred acres that Anthony had sold were awarded to Scarburgh. The fifty acres he had given to his son Richard were granted to another white planter, even though Richard, a free man, and his wife and children had lived on that land for five years.

Anthony Johnson's widow lived on at Tonies Vineyard for another decade until her own death. His sons managed to hold on to the rest of their property and their freedom, but they were increasingly threatened as more and more laws were passed to divide black "aliens" from the white majority. By 1682, major slave codes had been enacted in Virginia, denying slaves any of the privileges or rights accorded to white servants. Models of repression in the South for the next one hundred eighty years, Virginia's slave codes barred blacks from meeting in large numbers and from carrying arms, and they provided that slaves could be whipped for raising a hand to "any Christian" and killed if they ran away. When Anthony Johnson's grandson, John, Jr., died, he apparently left no one to carry on his name. No further records on the family have been found.

The story of Anthony Johnson and his family shows how the status of people of African heritage changed in the Chesapeake region as English colonization took root. With few exceptions, these changes mirror the transformations that took place in other areas of British colonial North America. There were major differences between northern and southern slavery, but in nearly every region people of African heritage enjoyed many more rights in the early colonial period than in the later.

Africans in
New Netherland

In 1612, merchants from Holland arrived on Manhattan Island and built a fur trading post, which became New Amsterdam. This trading post became one of the centers for the Dutch colony of New Netherland. The colony was operated by a corporation, the Dutch West India Company.

Slavery was introduced to New Netherland in 1626, when a Dutch ship arrived with eleven male Africans. Their last names may indicate their places of origin: Angola, Congo, Portugese, Santomee. Called "the company's people," they were brought to help build and fortify the settlement on Manhattan. Two years later, three female African slaves were brought to the colony from Angola.

Slavery in New Netherland was a kind of half-slavery. In contrast to other colonies, slaves there could be baptized and marry in the Dutch Reformed Church. The church also ordered "the instruction of Negroes in the Christian religion." Slaves in New Amsterdam could own property and go to court for the redress of wrongs.

One of the earliest cases of manumission, or freeing of slaves, occurred in New Amsterdam in 1644, when a dozen African men petitioned for their liberty on the grounds that they had served the colony well and should enjoy the fruits of their service. The Dutch authorities awarded them "conditional freedom" and later granted the men parcels of farmland outside the settlement. These land grants may not have been as generous as they appear; they were squarely in the path of any Indian march on New Amsterdam, and the colonial government counted on the Africans' desire to protect their property as a first line of defense for the city.

Slavery in New Netherland changed drastically after the English took over the colony in 1664 and renamed it New York. They agreed to respect Dutch property rights and to allow Dutch inhabitants to continue their religious practices and culture, but they did not respect the system of half-slavery. In the 1670s and 1680s, New York colonial officials strengthened the laws of bondage and granted masters complete power over their slaves. They ordered slaves to carry passes when they left their owners' homes and forbade them to travel on Sundays. They also curbed the rights of free blacks: One ordinance barred Africans and Indians from owning guns and prohibited more than four Africans or Indians from meeting together.

As Great Britain came to dominate the Atlantic slave trade, British merchants in New York seized the opportunity to profit by it. By 1746, one in five New Yorkers was of African descent. An official slave marketplace was established at what is now 60 Wall Street.

New York City also had many non-English white immigrants, for the city was a major Atlantic port with a diverse population even in Dutch times. As the number of white workers increased, there was growing pressure to keep blacks out of skilled crafts. In 1686, the city passed an ordinance stating that "noe Negroe or Slave be suffered to worke the bridges as a porter." In 1702, the city's white barrel-makers submitted a petition to the colonial assembly asking for protection against "breeding slaves to trades whereby honest and industrious tradesmen are reduced to poverty for want of employ."

Africans in the Colonies of New England

Not long after the *Mayflower* landed in 1620, Great Britain extended its holdings throughout the area of present-day Massachusetts. Later, England established other colonies on the northern coast of North America: New Hampshire in 1629, Connecticut in 1638, and Maine in 1639. Together, these colonies were called New England.

New England didn't have long growing seasons and its climate could not support large farms, so agriculture did not require a large workforce. As a result, the size of the slave population in this region was small. In 1679, the Connecticut colony's governor, William Leete, noted, "As for blacks, there comes sometimes three or four a year from Barbados." Blacks constituted only about two percent of the population of New England from the beginning to the end of the eighteenth century. Nevertheless, although there were fewer slaves in the New England colonies than elsewhere, slavery did exist throughout the region.

Blacks were clustered in coastal towns and large cities. Even in large population centers, however, their numbers remained small.

In a New England practice known as family slavery, young slave children

were often taken from their parents to be reared in white households and trained for business or family roles. John Watts of New York noted that slaves imported for the northern markets "must be young, the younger the better. . . . Males are best." Male slaves performed a wide diversity of jobs, and many were employed as assistants in their masters' businesses.

Young females were also in demand for training as house servants. Phillis Wheatley was only seven years old when she was transported from Africa in 1761. Taken into the Wheatley family of Boston that same year, she was taught to read and write by the Wheatleys' daughter and treated very much like a second daughter. Nine years after her arrival, her first volume of poetry was published—it was the first book published by an African American.

Although it was rare for a young slave to be treated as a member of the family quite as much as Phillis Wheatley was, close daily contact with the master's family and residence in the master's house gave slaves a fairly comfortable existence. In most cases, though, the social distance between master and slave was clearly marked. Even Phillis Wheatley, when invited to the homes of important whites after she had achieved fame, would politely decline to share their table and request to be seated instead at a side table set apart from the rest.

A few families and communities believed in Christianizing the slaves in their midst. Only three years after the first African arrived in New England, a slave woman belonging to Reverend John Stoughton became the first black convert. But few other conversions followed. The Protestant Church of England, the dominant religious authority in New England, actively discouraged slave efforts to adopt its faith. Slaves in New England were rarely baptized, and their marriages were never recognized.

Because of the nature of family slavery, a number of slaves in the region secured their freedom. But even as freemen, they were limited in their mobility, literacy, and personal freedom.

Africans in the Middle Atlantic Region

In 1655, the Dutch added to their North American holdings, taking over parts of present-day Pennsylvania, New Jersey, and Delaware from Sweden. But the Dutch had continuing difficulties in maintaining their North American outpost. By 1664, faced with the growing British presence in New England and the threat of British invasion, they ceded New Netherland to Great Britain in exchange for Suriname in South America. The British now controlled the Middle Atlantic region as well as New England.

As in New York, slaves in the Middle Atlantic region enjoyed few rights and privileges under British rule. Things changed in 1681, when the British crown granted William Penn proprietary rights to almost the entire area. Penn arrived the following year with a group from the Society of Friends, or Quakers, who had been a persecuted minority in England. Penn, also a Quaker, had suffered for his beliefs and viewed his colony as a holy experiment, a haven for all who were being persecuted. His constitution for the colony guaranteed religious freedom to all who believed in God and encouraged that slaves in the colony be freed. He also made a treaty with the chiefs of the Delaware Indian tribes, to ensure goodwill between the Native Americans and the European settlers.

Pennsylvania's liberal policies attracted a variety of religious sects, such as Lutherans and Mennonites, who had been persecuted for their beliefs in Germany. They, too, considered slavery immoral and against the laws of God. The first organized stand against slavery in the North American colonies was undertaken by a small group of Mennonites, who made an official protest that read, in part: "There is a saying that we should do to all men like as we will be done ourselves; making no difference of what generation, descent, or colour they are." Far more slaves were baptized in Pennsylvania than elsewhere in the colonies.

William Penn died in 1718, and unfortunately his heirs lacked his ethical values. By the middle 1720s, laws that placed restrictions on free blacks had been passed, and the legislators stated that "free negroes are an idle, slothful people . . . and afford ill examples to other negroes." In Pennsylvania, as elsewhere, economic needs overshadowed moral values.

Africans in South Carolina

The British claimed an area called Carolina as early as 1629. The northern and southern sections developed separately, and in 1729, Carolina was divided into North and South Carolina. Partly because of its longer growing season, South Carolina became the more prosperous of the two.

As in other colonies, for many years the terms *slave* and *servant* seem to have been used interchangeably in South Carolina. Both Indians and Africans, as well as whites, could serve indentures; it was not uncommon for a master to own all three. Merchant-planter John Smyth's South Carolina estate included nine Negroes, four Indians, and three whites in 1682. Nevertheless, between 1660 and 1710, planters slowly abandoned Indians and European indentured servants in favor of a labor force made up almost exclusively of slaves from Africa.

South Carolina's first cash crop was beef, and the industry was built on the labor of slave cattle herders. Slaves also established the colony's next cash crop—rice. Rice was not native to Europe or the Americas. The first rice seeds were brought from Africa, possibly by slaves. Slaves dug the rice fields and did the laborious work of planting, tending, and threshing the crop. By the early 1720s, rice cultivation had become the colony's leading occupation.

North American
Slavery in 1700

By 1700, the European-American population in the colonies had reached a quarter of a million. At twenty-eight thousand, the enslaved population totaled a little more than one-tenth that number; some twenty-three thousand lived in the South.

Although there were barely one thousand slaves in the New England colonies, and about four thousand in the colonies of the Middle Atlantic, the institution of slavery was by that time widely recognized by law. As early as 1641, the Puritan authorities in the Province of Massachusetts established a Body of Liberties that included the first statute to establish slavery in New England. Connecticut recognized slavery as a legal institution in 1650; Virginia did so in 1661; Maryland, in 1663; New York and New Jersey, in 1664 (the year the British took these regions from the Dutch); South Carolina, in 1682; Rhode Island and Pennsylvania, in 1700; and North Carolina, in 1715.

Many factors contributed to this change in the slaves' legal status, including the growing need for a cheap labor force. By 1700, the triangular trading voyage was an established institution: European slave traders sailed to Africa with cargoes of woolen or cotton goods, rum, brandy, iron bars, and glass beads.

They traded these goods for slaves, whom they transported to the West Indies, Newport, New York, Boston, and Charleston in what has become known as the Middle Passage. The ships then loaded up with sugar, tobacco, coffee, and timber and headed back to Europe. It was an extremely profitable business.

As more African slaves arrived in North America, people of European heritage began to fear alliances among Indians, Africans, and white indentured servants that might lead to slave revolts. This fear led to the creation of additional laws in every colony. As the years passed, slaves saw more and more of their rights taken away.

In the meantime, the first antislavery pamphlets were published by men who believed that slavery was against the laws of God. In 1693, a Quaker named George Keith published the first, entitled "An Exhortation and Caution to Friends Concerning Buying or Keeping of Negroes." The second, "The Selling of Joseph," by an English-born Bostonian named Samuel Sewall, was published in 1700. But these pamphlets were like cries in the wilderness. The vast majority of European Americans considered slavery part of the natural scheme.

Acceptance of slavery gave rise to laws that would be the basis for racial prejudice and oppression for the next two centuries. Soon all blacks were subjected to the same restrictions that governed slaves. In 1703, a law was passed in Massachusetts that required a master who freed a slave to pay a fee to the colony; another prohibited Indians and black servants from being on the streets after 9:00 P.M. In 1705, Virginia adopted a slave code that limited the number of slaves who could meet together at one time, restricted their travel, and forbade them to strike white persons or escape. That same code denied free blacks the right to testify in court against anyone but other blacks, and it forbade them to hold any office, "ecclesiastical, civil or military."

Africans
in Georgia

❦

Given the trends in the other twelve colonies, Georgia, the last of the thirteen British colonies in North America, was an oddity. Established in 1733 with the goal of aiding the English poor, Georgia was administered by a group of trustees, but James Oglethorpe was the only one actually to live in the colony. Effectively the colony's governor, Oglethorpe believed that slavery was "against the Gospel, as well as the fundamental law of England."

Oglethorpe was strongly influenced by a religious movement known as Methodism, which had broken away from the Protestant Church of England. Founded in England in the 1720s and '30s by John Wesley, Methodism sought to embrace all races and classes. When Wesley visited Georgia in 1735, as Oglethorpe's spiritual adviser, he brought his new faith to North America. Three years later, Wesley baptized the first black Methodist. Methodism would later become one of the most attractive faiths to America's blacks.

In January 1735, the trustees of Georgia passed a law banning the importation of blacks and prohibiting the use of blacks as slaves.

Georgia grew quickly. Soon, its original charity settlers, whose immigration

and settlement were financed by the trustees, were outnumbered by adventurers who paid their own way to make their fortunes exporting rice, indigo, lumber, beef, and pork. The need for slaves soon overrode the antislavery sentiments of James Oglethorpe. In 1750, just fifteen years after Oglethorpe had banned slavery in the colony, a new law was enacted making it lawful to import "Black Slaves or Negroes" to the province.

Two years after the passage of that law, the trustees relinquished control over the colony to the British crown, acknowledging the failure of the noble experiment. The laws of England governing slavery were much harsher than Georgia's had been. The 1755 English slave code, which ended the protection of a slave's life, listed numerous crimes for which slaves could be executed, placed severe restrictions on a slave's everyday movements, and made it very difficult for slaves to gain their freedom.

The Rise of the
Plantation Economy

Labor-intensive crops, such as rice in South Carolina, tobacco in Virginia, sugar in the lower Mississippi Valley, and later, cotton across the entire South, required hundreds, then thousands, and eventually tens of thousands of slaves. Even those areas not committed to growing crops on plantations became deeply involved in the plantation economy. Southern colonists who didn't run plantations still invested in them and supplied them with animals, food, technology, and slaves.

More and more often, new slaves were captured in the African interior and transported to Africa's west coast. The interior was the home of many hundreds of different "nations," each with its own language, religion, politics, social organization, and military tradition. About the only thing they had in common was that they tended to be farmers and herdsmen.

Atlantic Creole slaves had had some sense of the larger world through their contact with Europeans. Those from the interior of Africa, however, had no inkling of what lay beyond their own region. They were awed by the sight of the Atlantic Ocean. Many were so desperate not to be herded onto slave ships that they leaped into the tides and drowned themselves.

Those who survived the horrendous Middle Passage to the New World were cast among strangers, unable to communicate with anyone, wrenched from the crucial family, clan, and village ties that gave them their sense of identity. What must they have thought as they were unloaded at a North American port, crowded into slave pens, stripped and inspected for disease, then put up at auction blocks and sold to the highest bidder? Transported to a large plantation, herded into slave quarters, given a bit of food and clothing, and put straight to work in the fields, they did their best to find someone to show them what to do and to explain the rules for their new lives. The one thing they quickly understood was that the master was all-powerful and that any resistance would be met with punishment—often violent.

The plantation economy devoured slaves. Because thousands died from disease and overwork, more and more had to be imported. South Carolina, for example, had so many slaves, there was a black majority throughout most of the eighteenth century.

In areas with large numbers of black slaves, the whites lived in constant fear of revolts. Although the master of a large farm or plantation would sometimes teach one or two slaves reading, writing, and arithmetic in order to help with the farm's business, most masters discouraged slave literacy, since they believed that educated slaves tended to be restless. Dr. Francis Le Jau, an English minister, wrote home in 1707 that "the Negroes are generally very bad men, chiefly those that are Scholars. . . . Indians and Negroes shou'd [not] be . . . admitted to learn to read."

Planters felt that teaching slaves Christian faith might contribute, like education, to unrest. Planters also felt that only the master class could play or rest.

Unlike white immigrants, who were rewarded for personal initiative, free blacks were seen by many colonists as contributors to slave unrest, so the number of free blacks in plantation colonies was small. Free blacks often occupied a social no-man's-land: They had lost the protection of their masters but were denied opportunities for advancement. Still, a small number of free blacks prospered and in South Carolina even came to own slaves themselves. But by 1735, a South Carolina law required any newly freed person to leave the state within six months after gaining his or her freedom and also stated that any freed blacks who returned within seven years were to be reenslaved.

Slave Resistance

∞

While most African slaves struggled to adapt to their new lives in the North American colonies, a substantial number refused to accept their condition and ran away. White runaways were common as well. In 1735, a notice in the South Carolina *Gazette* announced: "Run away . . . two Irishmen Servants, both talking broad Scotch" and that two Negro men had run away at the same time.

There were many reasons for running away. A large percentage of advertisements for runaways revealed that they were African-born; many were "new negroes," blacks who had just arrived and hadn't yet been given names by their new masters. They may have believed that somehow they could find their way home. Juno, a girl of about fifteen who was "slender and strait Limb'd, and of the blackest Colour," arrived at Charleston, South Carolina, aboard the ship *Speaker* in June 1733. Within two weeks of being sold, she had disappeared.

Slaves were also spurred to run away when they were sold to a new owner. Many advertisements for runaways reported that they were "formerly the property of" someone else. Being sold to a new master often meant being separated from family and friends. In many cases fugitives reappeared after a time, having run away simply to visit family.

Most escaped slaves tried to get as far away from their masters as possible, and their destinations varied widely. It wasn't until the nineteenth century that north was the preferred direction. In 1728, in the woods near present-day Lexington, Virginia, a group of slaves managed to form a community that approximated an African village. They built homes like those they had known in Africa, established a tribal government under a man who had been a prince in the homeland, and used African farming techniques to grow crops. They lived this way for a year before local whites destroyed the village, killed the chief, and returned the other residents to their masters.

Many runaways were capable of navigating by the stars, and they escaped to all points of the compass. For fugitive slaves from South Carolina, traveling south was the best course. They made their way by foot and dugout canoe across the swamps and marshes of coastal Georgia to Florida, where the Spanish welcomed anyone fleeing their British enemies. In 1738, the Spanish governor of Florida gave these free people land for a town and fort two miles from St. Augustine.

Many runaways made their way to the port cities on the Atlantic Ocean. West was wilderness, almost inevitably inhabited by Indians. Although some Indians killed runaway slaves or reenslaved them or returned them to European settlers for a price, others welcomed and helped the fugitives.

Slave Revolts

Organized slave revolts in the colonial period were not as common as individual slave resistance. Nevertheless, they were a significant factor in colonial life. Most began as spontaneous acts of desperation by one slave. A particularly brutal beating, the selling of a spouse, or the withdrawal of a privilege could be the last straw. Sometimes, the defiant slave would prove to be a leader and become a rallying point for other dissident slaves.

In the early colonial period there were several instances of African slaves uniting with Indians. Africans and Indians invaded Hartford, Connecticut, in 1657 and threatened Virginia settlements seventy years later. Joshua Coffin, an early historian of slave insurrections, wrote this account in 1845: "[In the spring of 1690] Isaac Morrill, a native of New Jersey, came to Newbury [Massachusetts], to entice Indians and negroes to leave their masters and go with him, saying that *the English should be cut off, and the negroes should be free.* . . . Their intention was to take a vessel . . . for Canada and join the French against the English, and come down upon the backside of the country and save none but the negroes and Indians. . . ." The plot was discovered, and Morrill was arrested and sent to Ipswich, Massachusetts, for trial.

In 1712, twenty-seven armed slaves met in an orchard near the center of

New York City and set fire to an outbuilding. As whites arrived to put out the blaze, the slaves shot at them. Nine whites were killed before the militia was able to put down the revolt. The slave revolutionaries were quickly arrested, tried, and publicly executed. Colonial authorities then enacted extremely rigid slave codes.

Less than a dozen years later, in 1723, a series of suspicious fires in Boston led its citizens to believe a slave plot was to blame. The local militia was ordered out to police the city's slaves. A similar plot was reported in Burlington, Pennsylvania, in 1734.

In 1741, a suspicious fire that destroyed several buildings in New York City was also judged a slave conspiracy. A wave of hysteria shot through the city, and dozens of blacks and several Irish immigrants were arrested and tried. Many of the suspects—frightened people about to be executed—"confessed" to the existence of a plot to destroy the city. By the time the mass hysteria had spent itself, twenty-nine blacks, along with four white men and two white women who had been found guilty of aiding in the plot, had been either hanged or burned alive.

The Stono
Rebellion

South Carolina, with its majority slave population, was witness to the most stunning slave rebellion. In the early morning of Sunday, September 9, 1739, about twenty slaves, many of them Angolans led by a man named Cato (some sources give his name as Jemmy), gathered near the western branch of the Stono River, about twenty miles from Charleston. They broke into a storehouse, killed two guards, and made off with small arms and powder. They then marched south toward Florida, where they planned to join up with other runaways. Along the way, they burned houses and killed their occupants, reportedly sparing an innkeeper who was known for kindness to his slaves. Other slaves joined the band, some eagerly, some reluctantly. To the beating of drums, a flag was raised, and the marchers shouted, "Liberty!"

By the time the rebels had marched ten miles, they numbered between sixty and one hundred. In their wake lay twenty to forty dead white settlers, and "the Country thereabout was full of Flames." It was late on Sunday afternoon, and the rebels decided to set up camp in an open field.

Alarms had been raised throughout the countryside, and a force of armed and mounted planters attacked the rebels. Although the slaves boldly fought back, they were outgunned. Some were killed in the first volley; others were surrounded, questioned briefly, and then killed. Several who proved that they

had been forced to join the band were released. At least thirty slaves escaped, and during the next few days there was an intensive manhunt for them. Some were seized and shot—and according to one account, the planters "Cutt off their heads and set them up at every Mile Post they came to."

A small band of rebels managed to travel thirty miles south, but the militia caught up with them and, in the pitched battle that followed, either killed or dispersed them. Not until a full month later did the *Boston Weekly News-Letter* report that "the Rebellious Negros are quite stopt from doing any further Mischief, many of them having been put to the most cruel Death."

Maintaining African Traditions

It was said that Cato (or Jemmy) used his knowledge of drumming to "speak" to other African-born slaves and to call them to arms during the Stono Rebellion. The use of drums for communication was one African tradition that slaves in North America had maintained. Slaves were remarkably inventive in making percussion instruments out of tin pans, logs, and other available items. They also made stringed instruments out of horse-hair, animal skins or bladders, and gourds. For years, masters tolerated the music of their slaves, believing that it made them more content workers. But eventually they realized that slaves could communicate by means of intricate codes—the same drums that beat for dances and music could also beat a call for revolt. In some areas, slave drumming was outlawed, although that did not prevent the slaves from communicating through tapping their heels or slapping their hands on their bodies.

It was often a struggle even for slaves to keep their own names, since own-ers believed they could name their property. Occasionally an owner allowed his slaves to keep their names, especially if they were easy for him to pronounce. A South Carolina master who died before the American Revolution listed among his slaves Allahay, Banyky, Cumbo, Quash, Satirah, Tehu, and Temboy. Many Africans who had been named for the day of the week on which they were

born managed to hold on to their names in some form. Cuba was a female name for Wednesday; Cudjo (Monday) was often corrupted to Joe.

Olaudah Equiano, born in the area of present-day Biafra about 1745 and seized by slavers at the age of ten, told in his autobiography of the series of European names forced upon him:

"In this place I was called Jacob; but on board the *African Snow* I was called Michael. . . . On board [the *Industrious Bee*], my captain and master named me

Gustavus Vassa [after several famous kings of Sweden]. . . . When I refused to answer to my new name, which I at first did, it gained me many a cuff; so at length I submitted." Equiano purchased his freedom in 1766, and until his death in 1797 he worked actively to abolish the slave trade.

Another tradition that plantation slaves were able to maintain was music. They had a special style of singing, known as the call-and-response form, in which one person could make up new verses and the rest would answer as a chorus. Most slaves had Sundays off and were allowed to celebrate with music and dancing on Saturday nights. There were also times of community celebration, such as Christmas and harvesttime. Slaves used songs for religious purposes, as storytelling devices, and as a means of retaining their identities. One such song includes the verse: "Got one mind for white folks to see, / 'Nother for what I know is me, / He don't know, he don't know my mind."

The slaves were able to hold on to some aspects of their languages, even when they were placed with slaves who spoke different tongues. Although the words were different, many African languages shared common rules of grammar. Once slaves learned a few words of English, they were able to communicate with one another. In some areas, the resulting mix of English and African languages became almost a separate tongue. The best example of that can be found in the Sea Islands off the coast of South Carolina and Georgia, where a dialect called Gullah is still spoken.

African Contributions
to Colonial Society

A frican traditions of folklore and music influenced American ones in a major way. The folklore about witchcraft was often a blend, since African beliefs in witchcraft were fairly similar to European traditions. But in one area African beliefs were far more developed, and slaves proved influential: divination. Fortune-telling was a popular pastime among white colonists, but divination was different—like fortune-telling, it included the foretelling of future events, but it also used occult means to discover lost items or reveal culprits and thieves. In the Dutch colony of New Netherland, slaves were respected for their ability to foretell the weather.

Many slaves arrived from Africa with expertise in herbal medicine, and most colonial communities had at least one well-known slave herbalist who bought and sold roots and leaves and prescribed herbal medications.

Folktales, and especially tall tales, were an important African tradition that came to influence the European colonials. Many slaves used folklore to teach both their own children and their masters' children about life. Throughout the New World, blacks were known for their satiric wit, which they based on African traditions of improvisational humor. Often, their humor poked fun at European traditions. One slave gave the following response when his master proudly announced that when the slave died, he could be buried in the family

vault: "Me no care where me be buried; besides, Massa, suppose we be buried together, and de devil come looking for Massa, in de dark, he might take away poor Negro man in mistake."

Slaves introduced a number of musical instruments to the New World; among them were the banjo, the tambourine, and the three-stringed fiddle. Although fiddles were known to the European colonists, the style of energetic fiddling that became distinctly American has strong African influences.

Of course, the greatest contribution that African slaves made to colonial life was their work in building the new land that would eventually become a new nation. In the beginning, they and the enslaved Indians worked side by side with Europeans to establish the colonies. From New England to the Lower Mississippi, they built the forts, paved the streets, dug the canals, cleared the fields, grew the crops, and generally were involved in all areas of colonial commerce.

In the southern colonies, the herding and cattle-breeding skills of slaves were of great benefit. Their agricultural skills were crucial to the development of major cash crops, and they proved adept at cultivating rice. As the colonies grew, slave labor became more and more crucial to their economies, especially during times of war.

The Seven Years' War
and the
French and Indian Wars

Colonial America was constantly beset by armed conflict. Organized slave revolts not only affected the areas in which they occurred but also generated fear throughout the other colonies. But more serious threats to the British colonies were hostilities with the Indians and with other nations that also had interests in North America. Such battles occurred throughout the colonial era.

Many wars that affected the colonies were really campaigns in the worldwide struggle for empire between Great Britain and France, most notably the French and Indian Wars (1689–1763), a series of conflicts between the two powers in North America. The last of these wars broke out in 1755, when the British undertook an expedition against French forts in Canada and what is now upstate New York.

By 1756, the hostilities had become worldwide. Pitting Great Britain, Prussia, and Hanover against France, Russia, Austria, Saxony, and Sweden, battles were fought in Europe and India as well as in North America. In 1762, Spain entered the conflict on the side of France, but its late entry into the war did little to help France and caused Spain to lose its North American territories.

In the end, Great Britain triumphed. By signing the Treaty of Paris in 1763, France lost its possessions in North America and had to give Canada and all its territories east of the Mississippi River to Britain. Spain was forced to yield its territories in western Louisiana and Florida.

As wars disrupted the supply of European indentured servants to the colonies, and military enlistment siphoned off young white men from the labor force, the importance of slave workers increased. Especially after 1755, when the last of the French and Indian Wars drew thousands of young white men into the colonial armies, slaves made up the majority of the labor force, even in the northern colonies.

On the Eve of the American Revolution

Great Britain now controlled all of North America east of the Mississippi, from Canada to Florida. In addition to provinces in Canada and Florida, it could claim thirteen colonies.

In the north, economies based on fishing, small farming, and commerce—including the slave trade—grew steadily, with a dramatic increase in domestic and international trade.

In the southern colonies, small farms had given way to large plantations, with a population that was two-thirds black slaves. The need for an enslaved labor force had created a corresponding need to deny basic human rights to slaves. Southern plantation slavery had become *chattel* slavery: Slaves were no longer people, but property. They had no rights whatsoever.

Ironically, at the same time as African and African-American slaves were suffering the loss of even the most basic human rights in the colonies, the colonies themselves were beginning to demand more rights from England.

By the end of the eighteenth century, more and more colonists had come to resent the power of the British crown. More and more, they talked of liberty. Not just an ocean now separated them from Great Britain, but a new sense of a separate destiny. The colonists had become less dependent militarily and economically on the British and more free to concentrate on their own developing

country. They began to feel less like British subjects and more like Americans.

Many blacks shared those feelings. The descendants of people like Anthony Johnson could claim as long a lineage in America as the heirs of the first white colonists. As the years went on, more and more blacks, slave and free, began to feel that America was their home. Africa was as foreign to them as England was to the descendants of the first Pilgrims. Like the white colonists, black Americans had been pioneers in the new land. They, too, were Americans.

Milestones in the History of Blacks in Colonial America

1526   A Spanish settlement near present-day Georgetown, South Carolina, includes the first African slaves to settle in the New World.

1607   First permanent British settlement established at Jamestown, Virginia

1612   Merchants from Holland arrive on Manhattan Island and build a fort and a trading post that will become New Amsterdam.

1619   Twenty Africans arrive at Jamestown on a Dutch ship.

1621   First record of Anthony Johnson, a slave known as Antonio, in Jamestown

1626   Slavery is introduced to New Netherland when a Dutch ship arrives with twenty-six male Africans.

1638   Slave traders bring the first Africans to Boston, Massachusetts.

1641   The Province of Massachusetts enacts a statute establishing slavery—the first in New England. First marriage between slaves is recorded in New Amsterdam.

1644   A dozen enslaved Africans are manumitted (freed) and granted land in New Amsterdam.

1650   Connecticut recognizes slavery as a legal institution.

1651   Virginia grants Anthony Johnson 250 acres of land.

1657   A band of Africans and Indians invades Hartford, Connecticut.

1661   Virginia recognizes slavery as a legal institution.

1663   Maryland recognizes slavery as a legal institution.

1664   New York and New Jersey recognize slavery as a legal institution.

1665   Anthony Johnson and his wife move to Somerset County, Maryland.

1670   Anthony Johnson dies.

1681   British crown grants William Penn proprietary rights to the land that will become the Colony of Pennsylvania; its constitution guarantees freedom for slaves.

1682   Virginia enacts major slave codes. South Carolina recognizes slavery as a legal institution.

1686   New York City prohibits blacks from working with goods either imported into or exported from the city.

1689   The French and Indian Wars begin.

1690   Slaves revolt in Newbury, Massachusetts.

1693   Pennsylvania Quaker George Keith publishes the first antislavery pamphlet.

1700   The European population of the British colonies in North America is 250,000; the slave population is one tenth of that number. Rhode Island and Pennsylvania recognize slavery as a legal institution.

1703   Massachusetts requires masters who free slaves to pay a fee to the colony.

1705   Virginia adopts a restrictive slave code.

1712   Twenty-seven slaves revolt in New York City.

1715   North Carolina recognizes slavery as a legal institution.

1717   New London, Connecticut, denies free black Robert Jacklin the right to buy land.

1721   A series of suspicious fires in Boston arouses fears of a slave plot.

1727   Africans and Indians band together to threaten several Virginia settlements.

1728   A group of runaway slaves establishes a community near present-day Lexington, Virginia.

1734   A suspected slave plot in Boston

1735   Georgia passes a law banning the importation of slaves into the colony. A South Carolina law requires any newly freed person to leave the state within six months.

1738   The Spanish governor of Florida grants land near St. Augustine to escaped slaves from the British colonies, for a town and a fort.

1739   The Stono Rebellion occurs in South Carolina.

1741   A suspected slave conspiracy in New York City leads to the execution of twenty-nine blacks and six whites.

1746   One in five people in New York City is of African descent.

1750   Georgia recognizes slavery as a legal institution.

1755   Last of the French and Indian Wars breaks out; it is also known as the Seven Years' War.

1761   Seven-year-old Phillis Wheatley is transported from Africa to Boston.

1762   Spain enters the Seven Years' War on the side of France.

1763   Treaty of Paris signed, ending the Seven Years' War.

1770   Phillis Wheatley's book of poetry is published in England—the first book published by an African American.

Selected Bibliography

Berlin, Ira. *Many Thousands Gone: The First Two Centuries of Slavery in North America.* Cambridge, MA: The Belknap Press of Harvard University Press, 1998.

Ferguson, Leland. *Uncommon Ground: Archaeology and Early African America, 1650–1800.* Washington, D.C.: Smithsonian Institution Press, 1992.

Higgenbotham, A. Leon, Jr. *In the Matter of Color: Race & the American Legal Process: The Colonial Period.* New York: Oxford University Press, 1978.

Horton, James Oliver, and Lois E. Horton. *In Hope of Liberty: Culture, Community and Protest Among Northern Free Blacks, 1700–1860.* New York: Oxford University Press, 1997.

Johnson, Charles, Patricia Smith, and the WGBH Series Research Team. *Africans in America: America's Journey Through Slavery.* New York: Harcourt, Brace & Company, 1998.

Katz, William Loren. *Black Legacy: A History of New York's African Americans.* New York: Atheneum Books, 1997.

Piersen, William D. *Black Yankees: The Development of an Afro-American Subculture in Eighteenth-Century New England.* Amherst, MA: University of Massachusetts Press, 1988.

Wood, Peter H. *Black Majority: Negroes in Colonial South Carolina from 1670 Through the Stono Rebellion.* New York: Alfred A. Knopf, 1974.

Index